LIFE CYCLES

Tomatoes

by Robin Nelson

first step nonfiction

Lerner Publications Company · Minneapolis

This is a tomato.

There are many different kinds of tomatoes.

How do tomatoes grow?

A tomato seed is planted.

First, **roots** grow out of the seed.

Then a **shoot** pushes up through the dirt.

Now it is a **seedling**.

Leaves grow on the stem.

Then flower **buds** grow.

The yellow flowers open.

Bees fly to the flowers.

The flowers fall off, and the tomato grows.

A **ripe** tomato is red.

These tomatoes are ready to be picked.

New tomato seeds grow
inside the tomato.

Some seeds will be planted
to grow new tomatoes.

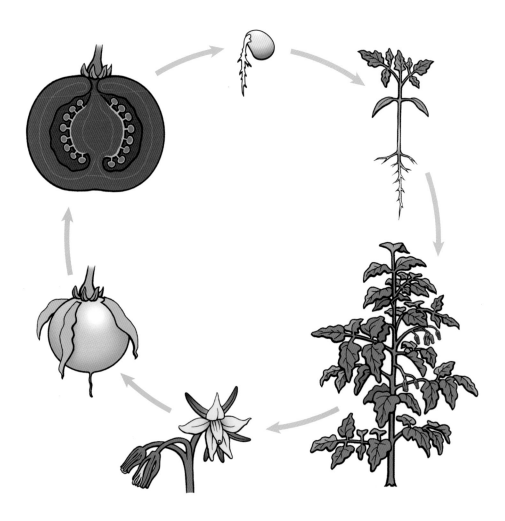

Tomatoes

Tomatoes come in many sizes and colors. Tomatoes are grown all over the world. California grows the most tomatoes in the United States.

The life cycle of a tomato is 55 to 85 days. This means seeds planted in the spring are ready to eat in the middle of the summer.

Tomato Facts

 Tomatoes are used to make ketchup and spaghetti sauce.

 Scientists say that tomatoes are a fruit because they have seeds. Some people say that tomatoes are a vegetable.

 Tomatoes are the world's most popular fruit.

 The United States grows more tomatoes than any other country.

Tomatoes are very good for you.

 Sometimes tomato plants need help to stand up because the tomatoes are so heavy. Gardeners use tomato cages to help support the plant.

 One tomato plant grows about 15 tomatoes each year.

Glossary

 buds – a flower that has not opened yet

 ripe – ready to eat

 roots – parts of a plant that grow down into the ground

 seedling – a young plant

 shoot – a plant that has just started to grow

Index

The images in this book are used with the permission of: © iStockphoto.com/dirkr, p. 2; © Dwight Kuhn, pp. 3, 8, 22 (second from bottom); © Paul Debois/Gap Photo/Visuals Unlimited, Inc., p. 4; © Todd Strand/Independent Picture Service, pp. 5, 6, 22 (center); © Client Ready Images/Jerome Wexler/Visuals Unlimited, Inc., pp. 7, 22 (bottom); © Elke Borkowski/ Visuals Unlimited, Inc., p. 9; © Julie Caruso/Independent Picture Service, pp. 10, 13, 14, 22 (top and second from top); © Marta Johnson, pp. 11, 16; © iStockphoto.com/DanDriedger, p. 12; © Melanie Acevedo/Jupiterimages, p. 15; © iStockphoto.com/Ridofranz, p. 17; illustrations by © Laura Westlund/Independent Picture Service.
Front cover: © iStockphoto.com/John Cooke.

Lerner Publications Company
A division of Lerner Publishing Group, Inc.
241 First Avenue North
Minneapolis, MN 55401 U.S.A.

Website address: www.lernerbooks.com

Library of Congress Cataloging-in-Publication Data

Nelson, Robin, 1971–
        Tomatoes / by Robin Nelson.
            p.   cm. — (First step nonfiction. Plant life cycles)
        Includes index.
        ISBN: 978–0–7613–4070–6 (lib. bdg. : alk. paper)
        1. Tomatoes—Life cycles—Juvenile literature. I. Title. II. Series.
    SB349.N45 2009
        635'.642—dc22   2008033748

Manufactured in the United States of America
1 2 3 4 5 6 – DP – 14 13 12 11 10 09